Outrun the Shadow © 2023 Nancy

All rights reserved.

No part of this publication may be reproduced, stored in a retrieval system, or transmitted, in any form or by any means, electronic, mechanical, photocopying, recording or otherwise, without the prior written permission of the presenters.

Nancy Cowan asserts the moral right to be identified as author of this work.

Presentation by *BookLeaf Publishing*

Web: www.bookleafpub.com

E-mail: info@bookleafpub.com

ISBN: 9789358317596

First edition 2023

Outrun the Shadow

Nancy Cowan

For my two little heartbeats.

To everyone who showed us love, hope and support in any way... I hope you know how grateful we are.

ACKNOWLEDGEMENT

Thanks to those who encouraged me to own and write my story.

PREFACE

Never take anything for granted. Your life, what you know to be true and what you hold dear can be destroyed in a second... by that one phone call.
These poems show how I faced my biggest fears and rebuilt a new life for myself and my two little heartbeats, despite everything.

The Shadow

He sat there in the midst of my sleepless night.
I sensed his shadow before I saw him.
A black entity whose presence controlled the longest night.
The looming and lurking figure hiding the ego of the man I once knew.
His cloak of arrogance hiding the truth.
A heart of darkness manipulating the one he promised to love.
A labyrinth of lies to conceal his true nature.
Words of warning like daggers silencing me.
For how long?
His shadow did fade to reveal a man exposed for what he had done to his family.

The Glass Case

Into the glass case I placed my broken heart.
A place to keep it safe until I could deal with the pain.
Days tumbled into one another as I tried to fix it all.
My heart would have to wait.

Months trawled on like an endless night,
My bruised and broken heart still in its case,
It lay scorched and scarred bearing the weight of love's bitter fate.
The glass case was a shield from the world outside.

But one day the case began to crack.
From somewhere my strength was coming back,
A raging battle began to ignite a path to healing.
I wanted to end the black night.

The glass case had guarded my wounds.
Slowly it started to crack.
With each new day courage and strength grew,
Each shard teaching me a lesson.

Slowly the glass case grew frail.

I didn't need it anymore.
A stronger heart was being reborn.
Resilience and courage—my guides.

A tapestry of healing, of breaking the case.
Acknowledging the pain and embracing the story.
Speaking it out loud and empowering my heart,
Was perhaps the greatest lesson of rebuilding my heart.

Buried Truth

Yes I buried it.
Swallowed it whole.
Kept my mouth shut.
Dried my tears.
Tried to still the tempest inside me.
I put on a convincing show.
Told everyone I was fine.
My mask and practiced smile worn each day,
Whilst inside I was slowly dying.
With each step I took the ground shook.
Nothing could ease the feeling.
The effort it took to hide the truth with every sinew of my being.
Slowly, slowly the buried truth began to emerge from its grave.
Uncovered and exposed the shame began to creep in.
A lesson learned.

The "Victim"

In the guise of a "victim", he stood so tall.
The narcissistic mask, a master of the fall.
Through conversations filled with manipulative charm,
He deceived and disguised his truth.

Using me like a shield,
He played me like a puppet,
The charade I had to act out.
To hide the truth with lies.

Behind this façade,
He began to weave his web,
Controlling and manipulating to make others believe,
That he'd done nothing wrong.

Behind the curtain the truth lay hidden,
Me and the two little heartbeats trapped in the guise,
Little by little the truth started to emerge,
The curtain was lifting, hanging off its rail.

The light was exposing the shadow's lies,
The truth was out.

Time for shielding was over for us.
Now everyone could see him for what he was.

The "victim's" mask crumbled exposing his web of lies.

The Wasteland

And so I found myself in the wasteland's grasp,
My life undone,
I stumbled through dust-laden echoes of a past now gone,
A once vibrant life, now marred and uncertain.

Falling amid shadows, my memories decayed.
Tainted in the remnants of my darkest dreams, lost in disarray.
My footsteps faltered as I danced with despair.

Through the debris of a life now estranged, a symphony of sorrow, forever unchanged.
In the wasteland's embrace, hopes are thrust,
A tragic ballet in the ashes of trust.

No Place Like Home

No place like home...or so they say,
Yet as I stood outside, a paradox was at play.
Dread lingered in my bones as I crossed the threshold's thorny embrace,
Yearning to escape from this familiar space.

Behind closed doors, secrets unfolded.
Smoke and mirrors maintained, a story retold.
All my emotions repressed,
A home once warm, now a heartache's nest.

The doorstep echoes a silent plea,
To be anywhere but home, yet here is where I was forced to be.
Pretending it's fine, masking the ache,
A painted smile, a façade to make.

The Friend

Thank you for answering my call that day.
Thank you for reminding me of all my qualities.
Thank you for just holding me there with your love.
Thank you for checking in through all the days in-between when everything was muddy.
You will never know how much your friendship saved me.

Space

It gave me space.
It didn't speak to me.
It didn't come near me.
It barely acknowledged my existence.
It said it was giving me "space".
SPACE!
I didn't need space.
I didn't need your silence.
I didn't need your time.
I needed you to be truthful.
And you showed me I wasn't good enough, even for that.

The Storm

The wind battered the trees that night.
So ferocious were my feelings of anger.
The rain slashed the window panes.
So hot were the tears of despair I cried.
The sound of the gale so turbulent outside.
So mirroring my anxious heartbeat.
The trees bent double by the weight of the wind.
So were the lies twisted on your tongue.
Relentless hammering rain on the roof.
So I gave my ring back to you.

The Marionette

The play began.
I turned up everyday to the theatre.
Unsure of my lines.
Unsure of my role.
Allowing him to set the scene.
He gave me my lines as I became his marionette.
Moved this way and that.
His hands held the strings of control so tight.
A puppet without a soul who moved at his will.
My life in his grip.
But one day I gathered my strength
I took the scissors and sliced the strings.
Suddenly the spotlight on his stage grew dim.
Now he had no one to control or to use to hide his soul.
He fled.

Brave?

You are so brave.
- Don't feel it.
How did you do it?
- I had no choice.
Why didn't you tell me?
- I was too ashamed.
I could have helped.
- I wouldn't have known what to ask you for.
Can't you see how brave you are?
-Maybe one day. I just hope I did my best.

Navigating

Beneath the canvas of the midnight sky,
The nightmare unfolds, as stars align high.
Long nights of navigating love's eclipse,
A breakup's journey the only script.

In the quiet moments, trying to explain,
To the two little heartbeats, the shift, the subtle pain.
Stars as witnesses to words gently said,
Navigating through the tears they shed.

A celestial guide, in the velvet night,
Finding a path, embracing the light.
Through the labyrinth of emotions untold,
A compass of stars, our new story unfolds.

Each constellation, a chapter to turn,
In the breakup's script, a lesson to learn.
The night, a canvas, where resilience gleams,
Navigating the echoes of shattered dreams.

The stars, timeless witnesses of the night,
Guide the journey, as darkness takes flight.
In the long nights, love's constellations glow,
Navigating a breakup, allowing hearts to grow.

Kindness

I have never known kindness like it.
Food.
Shelter.
A place to retreat.
Trailer loads of logs to keep us warm.
Bills paid.
TV reinstated.
A car so we didn't need to worry.
Words of support.
Wine nights.
Mindfulness boxes.
Tea made for us.
Christmas presents were given to us so the two heartbeats got presents.
Days of fun.
Cards with words of encouragement.
Messages.
Cups of coffee.
Listening ears.
Tissues.
People I could speak to even at 2 am.
Love, love and more love to mend all the brokenness.
And so many more random acts of kindness that just made it all a little easier.
Thank you won't ever seem enough.

My Tribe

Together they held me.
Reminded me of who I am.
Inspired me in so many ways.
Because of them I survived.
Every day I give thanks for them.

Your childhood in my hands

In the aftermath of my family's demise,
Life stretches on, beneath the skies.
The break-up's weight, too heavy to bear,
Yet, for the two little heartbeats I had to prepare.

In the hands that cradled dreams so small,
Their childhood's essence,
I must carefully install.
Amidst the shards of what once was,
I had to weave a tale, build bridges across.

Through tear-streaked nights and days so long,
Somehow I found the strength to carry on.
Their laughter, a beacon in the gloom,
Guiding me through the heartbreak's room.

For in my hands, their childhoods rest,
A sacred duty, a nurturing quest.
To mend the wounds, to heal, to soothe,
To build a haven where love will prove.

In every sunrise, a promise anew,
To paint their world in a brighter hue.
Though shadows linger from the past,
My love, resilient, will forever last.

Mama Bear

I can't promise there won't be tough days but...
I will fight for you so you know you have been heard.
I will support you as you try to untangle the world you thought you knew and make sense of the new one.
I will teach you how to stand up for yourself.
I will teach you how to walk through even the blackest of nights.
I will empower you to be truly and wholly who you are and to love who you are.
I will show you how to love and be loved even when you have been hurt.
And through it all I hope you hold onto just how wonderful you are.

Rebuilding

How do you rebuild an entire life?
How do you take the ashes from the fire and rise like a phoenix?
How do you try to explain why it all went wrong?
How do you fashion out of the cold, damp clay, the life that had been trodden on?
How do you piece together the shattered hopes and dreams?
How do you begin again?

Little by little.
Tear by tear.
Stone by stone.
Step by step.

Starting with a strong foundation.
Dug deep into the solid rock.
Held tight by the bonds that will never break.
Slowly, steadily, securely.
With help from people who pass you the bricks,
Who pour the concrete,
Who wait with you as it sets,
Who check with you to make sure it's set,
Who offer advice,

Who show you new ways of thinking about it,
Who turn your face towards the sun.

Rebuilding—tears, tantrums, frustrations, swear words, grief, loss.
Rebuilding— trust, hope, a future, love beyond measure and healing.

Hold On

Just one more turn in the road.
- I can't.
Just one more sunset.
- I'm too tired.
Just one more climb.
- I don't have the strength.
It's there just you wait until you see.
- I don't have faith.
You have to let hope be your guiding light.

Happy

And one day my smile came back.
But this time my eyes smiled too.
This time happiness was at the core of my being.
Happiness radiated from within even when my face didn't smile it.
I embodied it.
Happiness.

Together

Together we are stronger than ever.
Together we are rebuilding.
Together we are laughing again.
Together we are smiling more often.
Together we know we have each other.
Together we are enjoying life again.
Together we are living through all the emotions and holding each other's hearts.
Together forever, my two little heartbeats and I.
Growing, living, loving and forever grateful for the graces and kindnesses shown to us.
Together paying it forward, little by little.

Milton Keynes UK
Ingram Content Group UK Ltd.
UKHW020940220424
441551UK00019B/1461

9 789358 317596